# Xtreme Adventure

# GHOST HUNTING

### BY S.L. HAMILTON

EDGE
FRANKLIN WATTS

LONDON•SYDNEY

This edition first published in 2015 by
Franklin Watts
338 Euston Road
London NW1 3BH

Franklin Watts Australia
Level 17/207 Kent Street
Sydney NSW 2000

Copyright © 2014 by Abdo Consulting Group, Inc.

First published in the USA by ABDO Publishing Company.

Editor: John Hamilton
Graphic Design: Sue Hamilton
Cover Design: Sue Hamilton

Acknowledgements:
Cover Photo: Thinkstock.
Interior Photos: Alamy-pgs 10-11; AP-pgs 4-5, 7 (inset) 12-13, 20-23, & 26-27 (bottom);
Bourbon Orleans Hotel-pgs 16-17; Corbis-pg 29; Dreamstime-pg 28; iStock-pgs 6-7 & 8-9;
Library of Congress-pg 22 (inset); Matt Smith-pgs 18-19; Thinkstock-pgs 1, 2-3, 14-15; 18
(inset), 24-25, 26-27 (top); 30-32; Winchester Mystery House-pg 11 (inset).

Every attempt has been made to clear copyright. Should there be any inadvertent
omission please apply to the publisher for rectification.

A CIP catalogue record for this book is available from the British Library.

Dewey Classification: 133.1

(HB) ISBN: 978 1 4451 4041 4
(Library ebook) ISBN: 978 1 4451 4044 5

Printed in China

Franklin Watts is a division of Hachette
Children's Books, an Hachette UK company.
www.hachette.co.uk

# CONTENTS

Ghost Hunting . . . . . . . . . . . . . . . . . . . . . . . .4

Tools & Equipment . . . . . . . . . . . . . . . . . . . . .6

Dangers . . . . . . . . . . . . . . . . . . . . . . . . . . .8

Haunted Houses. . . . . . . . . . . . . . . . . . . . . . .10

Ghost Hotels . . . . . . . . . . . . . . . . . . . . . . . .14

Haunted Hospitals . . . . . . . . . . . . . . . . . . . .18

Battlegrounds . . . . . . . . . . . . . . . . . . . . . . .22

Ships . . . . . . . . . . . . . . . . . . . . . . . . . . . . .26

Cemeteries . . . . . . . . . . . . . . . . . . . . . . . . .28

Glossary. . . . . . . . . . . . . . . . . . . . . . . . . . .30

Index . . . . . . . . . . . . . . . . . . . . . . . . . . . . .32

# GHOST HUNTING

Some people say there are no such things as ghosts. Others are sure these spirits of the dead are real. They describe ghosts in many different ways. Some ghosts make loud moans and howls, while others are quiet. Some have clear shapes, while others are light wisps of smoke. Some ghosts seem friendly, while others are terrifying.

*XTREME FACT – Ghosts are also called spirits, wraiths, spectres, apparitions, phantoms and spooks.*

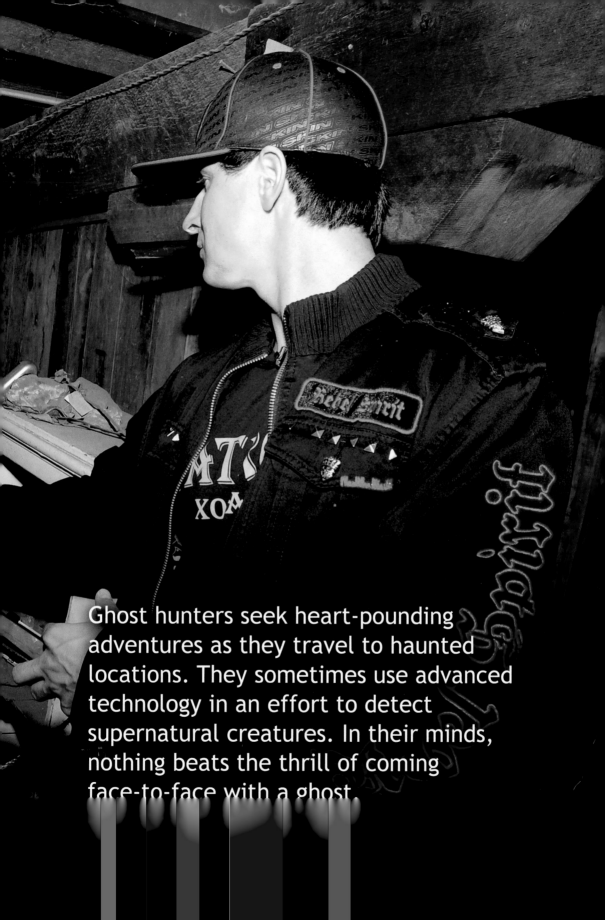

Ghost hunters seek heart-pounding adventures as they travel to haunted locations. They sometimes use advanced technology in an effort to detect supernatural creatures. In their minds, nothing beats the thrill of coming face-to-face with a ghost.

# TOOLS & EQUIPMENT

Ghost hunters use temperature-sensing equipment, such as thermal scanners and thermometers, to find cold spots. These cool areas could be a ghostly presence. A thermal image shows the shape and size of a cold mass.

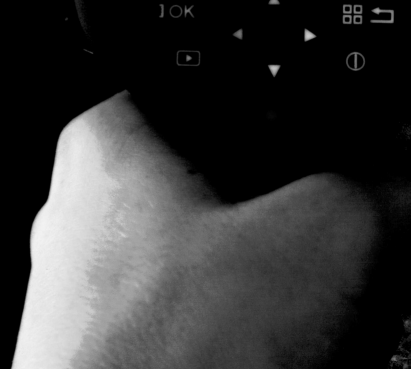

Ghost hunters also use motion detectors, cameras and digital sound recorders in their searches.

*A ghost hunter listens for electronic voice phenomena (EVP) evidence of a spirit, in a recording made in a cemetery.*

**XTREME FACT** – Ghost hunters often carry GPS units or compasses to help them find their destination.

# DANGERS

Ghost hunters sometimes get injured while exploring dangerously neglected buildings and cemeteries. Damaged floors, stairs and windows often cause falls. Walking or running on uneven ground can cause sprained ankles and broken bones. Ghost hunters must stay alert to protect themselves from their surroundings.

*XTREME FACT – It is possible to be scared to death. When frightened, the human body produces a large amount of adrenaline. This chemical typically helps a person survive a life-threatening situation. However, in a few cases, it may cause the heart to get off rhythm or even stop beating.*

# HAUNTED HOUSES

Ghost hunters often seek old, abandoned homes as likely locations for finding spirits. However, well-kept homes may also have ghostly presences. Some call the Winchester Mystery House in San Jose, California (below), one of the most haunted homes in the USA.

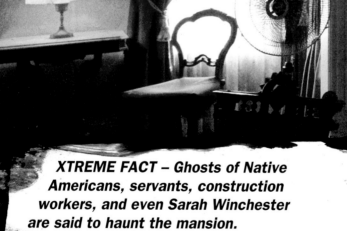

**XTREME FACT** – *Ghosts of Native Americans, servants, construction workers, and even Sarah Winchester are said to haunt the mansion.*

Sarah Winchester started construction of the mansion after her husband and daughter died. A psychic told her that ghosts were seeking revenge and that she needed to build a house to keep them happy. Work began in 1884 until Sarah's death in 1922. Today, visitors tour the mansion's 160 rooms, secret passages, stairs that go nowhere, and doors that open to walls, all designed by Sarah to keep herself safe from vengeful spirits.

The White House, home of the US President, has many stories of hauntings. President Lincoln (1809-65) has reportedly been seen standing at a window, sitting on a bed, and even wandering the hallways. The president's son, Willie, who died in 1862 at the age of 11, is said to still giggle and run up and down the haunted hallways of the White House.

The attic above the president's office has a history of unexplained noises. David Burns, the original owner of the White House land, is said to haunt the attic along with the ghost of William Henry Harrison. He was the ninth US President, and the first president to die in office, in 1841, after serving only a month.

**XTREME FACT–** During the War of 1812, British soldiers set fire to the White House and the US Capitol building. The ghost of a British soldier with a burning torch is said to haunt the White House to this day.

# GHOST HOTELS

Hotels are often known for their ghostly guests. The Ettington Park Hotel in Warwickshire is one of the most haunted hotels in the UK. Ghost hunters, visitors and staff members have all told of spirited encounters there.

The ghost of 'Lady Emma' is the hotel's most popular spirit. She is reportedly dressed in a white gown and glides along the hotel corridors at night. Other ghostly sightings include a monk, the Shirley boys (who drowned in the River Stour in the 1800s), a man and his dog, a grey lady and an army officer.

**XTREME FACT** – *Horror novelist Stephen King was inspired to write* The Shining *after a stay at the Stanley Hotel, a famous haunted hotel in the USA.*

Bourbon Orleans Hotel
is in New Orleans, USA.
It features a grand ballroom,
a spiral staircase, chandeliers
and ghosts. In the 1800s, the
site held a ballroom and theatre,
and then a convent, before it
became a hotel. Visitors claim
to have seen the spirits of a
little boy and girl, a soldier,
nuns and a ghostly dancer.

**XTREME FACT – Haunted
hotels often have resident
psychics. They try to
communicate with the
hotel's spirits.**

Many people claim to have seen a lone ghost dancer in the Bourbon Orleans Hotel's beautiful ballroom, dancing below the crystal chandeliers.

# HAUNTED HOSPITALS

Hospitals seem to hold restless spirits. Waverly Hills Sanatorium in Louisville, USA, is an abandoned hospital with stories of paranormal activities. Ghost hunters look for the spirits of nurses and patients, as well as ghosts of a little boy bouncing a ball and a little girl playing hide-and-seek.

Some witnesses hear strange voices, moans and cries. There are also reports of hot and cold spots, unusual lights, orbs and shadows. Are they the former residents and staff of the hospital?

**XTREME FACT** – Waverly Hills used a tunnel to take away the bodies of dead patients. It was given the nickname 'Death Tunnel'. People sometimes see a ghostly horse-drawn hearse arriving at the entrance to the tunnel.

...ham Park Hospital in Liverpool ...ed in 1954 to treat patients with ...e mental problems. Before this, ...1874, the building housed an ...nage for the children of sailors ...t sea.

*XTREME FACT – Newsham Park Hospital is so popular with ghost hunters that tour companies have an 18-month waiting list for people wanting to book a visit!*

It is believed a little ghost spotted upstairs may be the spirit of a boy. He died after being locked inside a small cupboard as a punishment. The bodies of over 16,000 orphans were cremated at Newsham.

# BATTLEGROUNDS

After the Battle of Hastings in 1066, an abbey was built on Senlac Hill. It is said to mark the place where King Harold II was killed. The abbey is now mostly in ruins, but there have been unexplained sightings there.

A soldier carrying a sword was seen in the Great Hall, and a group of visiting school children saw a man dressed in a monk's robe. They thought he was a re-enactor. It was only later that they found out there were no re-enactors at the abbey that day!

**XTREME FACT –**
*Historians believe that around 10,000 soldiers were killed at the Battle of Hastings.*

The Alamo is a fort in San Antonio, USA. In 1836, it was the site of a bloody battle between Mexican soldiers and American settlers. After two weeks of fighting, more than 250 settlers were dead, along with around 600 Mexican soldiers killed or injured. The Alamo's history of ghostly tales began shortly after the battle.

**XTREME FACT –** In 1836, after the battle, Mexican soldiers were ordered to destroy the Alamo. One story says that as they approached the church (right), they were stopped by a ghostly figure holding a fireball. The soldiers turned and ran away!

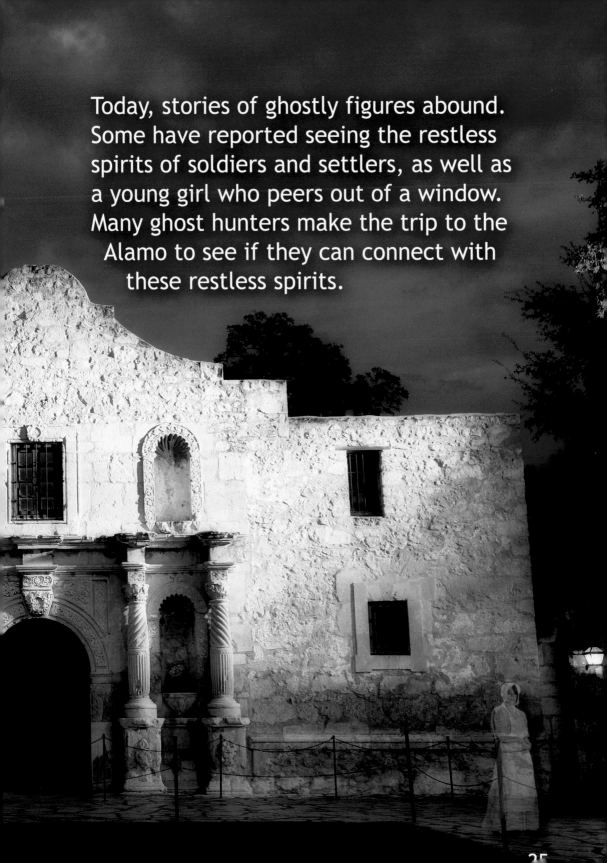

Today, stories of ghostly figures abound. Some have reported seeing the restless spirits of soldiers and settlers, as well as a young girl who peers out of a window. Many ghost hunters make the trip to the Alamo to see if they can connect with these restless spirits.

# SHIPS

The *Queen Mary* is a retired ocean liner, first launched in 1934. Today, the ship is a hotel and restaurant. It is known as 'the haunted ship'.

The USS *Hornet* is a US aircraft carrier first launched in 1943. The great warship had many successes, but also suffered several tragedies. More than 300 sailors died on the *Hornet*. Today, the ship is a National Historic Landmark and a museum in Alameda, USA. Ghost hunters visit the ship trying to find spectral crewmen.

The ghost of a crewman, accidentally crushed by watertight door #13, has been spotted below decks. The first-class swimming pool also sports ghostly activity, with wet footprints and splashing noises reported even when the pool area is supposedly empty.

Some USS Hornet staff and visitors report seeing or hearing spectral sailors. The spirit crew work, talk, drop tools, open and close hatches, flush toilets, and continue to carry out their ghostly orders.

# CEMETERIES

Cemeteries are popular locations for ghost hunting. Greyfriars Kirkyard, Edinburgh, is well known for its ghostly occupants. The cemetery opened in the 1560s. It is said that the ghost of George MacKenzie haunts an area of the graveyard called the Covenanters Prison. MacKenzie's ghost has attacked visitors, giving them bruises and scratches.

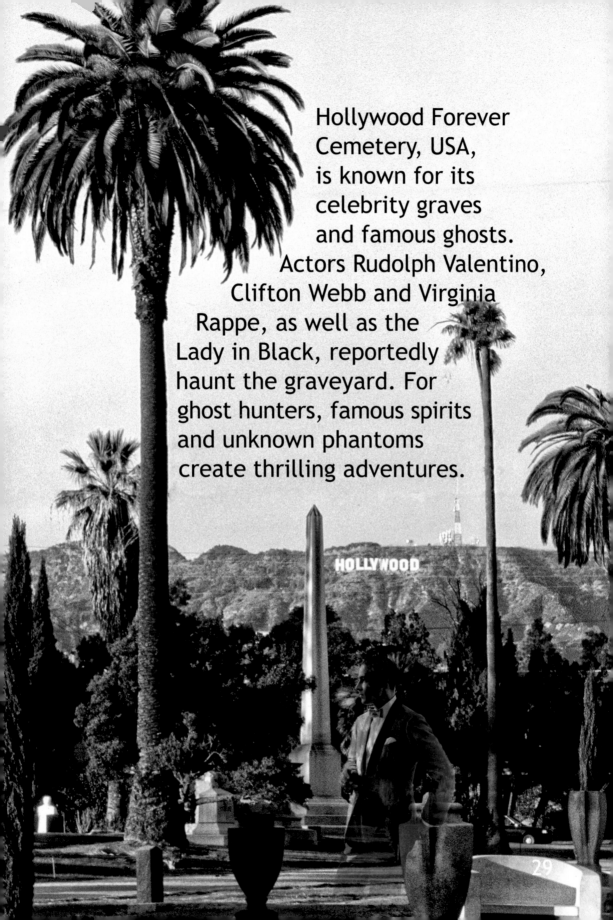

Hollywood Forever Cemetery, USA, is known for its celebrity graves and famous ghosts. Actors Rudolph Valentino, Clifton Webb and Virginia Rappe, as well as the Lady in Black, reportedly haunt the graveyard. For ghost hunters, famous spirits and unknown phantoms create thrilling adventures.

# GLOSSARY

ADRENALINE
A chemical created in the human body that is released when a person feels strong emotions such as fear or excitement. Adrenaline causes the heart to beat faster and gives a person a quick burst of energy.

APPARITION
A ghostlike image of a person or object; a supernatural appearance.

CREMATED
Burning a body after death, often in a special oven, turning it to ashes.

ELECTRONIC VOICE PHENOMENA (EVP)
Sounds found on audio recordings that are believed to be the voices or sounds of ghosts or spirits. EVP may also be caused by static, radio transmissions, and background noise in the area of the recording.

GPS
(GLOBAL POSITIONING SYSTEM)
A system used to pinpoint where a person is located based on satellite tracking.

## PARANORMAL
A force or experience that cannot be immediately explained by science.

## PSYCHIC
A person who claims to have an extraordinary understanding of, and connection to, supernatural forces and influences, such as ghosts. Also known as a medium or clairvoyant.

## RE-ENACTOR
A person who takes part in modern re-enactments of historical events. They wear clothes and use tools and weapons from the period.

## SUPERNATURAL
A being, force, or event that defies the laws of nature.

## THERMAL SCANNER
A heat-sensitive device that displays the different surface temperatures of whatever it is pointed at. Warmer temperatures are shown in red colours, while cooler temperatures are in blue colours.

# INDEX

**A**
adrenaline 8
Alamo, the 24, 25
American settlers 24

**B**
Battle of Hastings 22, 23
Bourbon Orleans Hotel 16, 17
Burns, David 13

**C**
camera 7
Capitol (building), US 13
compass 7

**D**
Death Tunnel 19
digital sound recorder 7

**E**
Edinburgh 28
electronic voice phenomena (EVP) 7
Ettington Park Hotel 14, 15

**G**
GPS unit 7
Greyfriars Kirkyard 28

**H**
Harrison, William Henry 13
Hollywood Forever Cemetery 29
*Hornet,* USS 26, 27

**K**
King, Stephen 14
King Harold II 22

**L**
Lady Emma 15
Lady in Black 29
Lincoln, Abraham 12
Lincoln, Willie 12
Liverpool 20
Louisville, Kentucky 18

**M**
MacKenzie, George 28
Mexican soldiers 24
monks 15, 23
motion detector 7

**N**
National Historic Landmark 26
New Orleans, Louisana 16
Newsham Park Hospital 20, 21

**O**
orphans 20, 21

**P**
psychic 11, 16

**Q**
*Queen Mary* 26

**R**
Rappe, Virginia 29

**S**
San Antonio, Texas 24
San Jose, California 10
Senlac Hill 22
*Shining, The* 14
Shirley Boys, the 15
Stanley Hotel 14

**T**
thermal scanner 6
thermometer 6

**U**
USA 10, 12, 13, 14, 16, 18, 24, 29

**V**
Valentino, Rudolph 29

**W**
War of 1812 13
Waverly Hills Sanatorium 18, 19
Webb, Clifton 29
White House 12, 13
Winchester, Sarah 10, 11
Winchester Mystery House 10